Cryptocurrency Unveiled: An Introductory Guide to Understanding and Trading Digital Assets

Copyright © 2010 by Traders Speak

All rights reserved. No part of this publication may be reproduced, distributed, or transmitted in any form or by any means, including photocopying, recording, or other electronic or mechanical methods, without the prior written permission of the publisher, except in the case of brief quotations embodied in critical reviews and certain other noncommercial uses permitted by copyright law.

Title: Cryptocurrency Unveiled: An Introductory Guide to Understanding and Trading Digital Assets

Table of Contents

Introduction

Chapter 1: What is Cryptocurrency?

Chapter 2: Understanding Blockchain Technology

Chapter 3: Getting Started with Cryptocurrency

Chapter 4: Types of Cryptocurrencies

Chapter 5: How to Choose a Cryptocurrency Exchange

Chapter 6: Setting Up Your Cryptocurrency Wallet

Chapter 7: Buying and Selling Cryptocurrency

Chapter 8: Security Measures for Cryptocurrency

Chapter 9: Cryptocurrency Trading Strategies

Chapter 10: Risks and Challenges in Cryptocurrency Trading

Chapter 11: Regulatory Environment and Taxation

Chapter 12: The Future of Cryptocurrency

Conclusion

Glossary

Resources

Introduction

Introduction: Navigating the Dynamic World of Cryptocurrency

Welcome to "Cryptocurrency Unveiled: An Introductory Guide to Understanding and Trading Digital Assets." In this comprehensive book, we embark on a journey through the fascinating realm of cryptocurrency, unraveling its complexities, exploring its potential, and equipping you with the knowledge and tools to navigate the exciting world of digital assets.

The rise of cryptocurrency over the past decade has captured the imagination of individuals, investors, and innovators worldwide. Born out of the desire for a decentralized and borderless form of money, cryptocurrencies have evolved from a niche concept to a global phenomenon, challenging traditional financial systems and reshaping the way we perceive and interact with money.

In this introductory guide, we embark on a quest to unravel the mysteries of cryptocurrency, starting with the fundamentals. We delve into the concept of cryptocurrency, defining what it is, how it works, and why it matters in today's digital age. From the pioneering Bitcoin to the myriad of alternative coins (altcoins) and tokens that populate the cryptocurrency landscape, we explore the diversity of digital assets and their unique features and use cases.

But cryptocurrency is more than just digital money—it's a technological marvel built on the foundations of blockchain technology. Blockchain serves as the underlying infrastructure that powers cryptocurrencies, providing a decentralized and transparent ledger for recording transactions without the need for intermediaries. We dissect the inner workings of blockchain, unraveling its intricacies, and exploring its potential to revolutionize not just finance but myriad other industries.

Armed with a solid understanding of cryptocurrency and blockchain technology, we guide you through the practical aspects of entering the world of digital assets. From choosing a reputable cryptocurrency exchange to setting up a secure wallet and executing buy and sell orders, we provide step-by-step guidance to help you navigate the complexities of cryptocurrency trading with confidence.

But with great opportunity comes great risk, and the world of cryptocurrency is no exception. Throughout this guide, we shine a spotlight on the various risks and challenges associated with cryptocurrency trading, from market volatility and regulatory uncertainty to security threats and technological vulnerabilities. We equip you with essential risk management strategies and best practices to safeguard your investments and navigate the unpredictable terrain of the cryptocurrency market.

As we journey through the pages of this book, we also peer into the future of cryptocurrency, exploring emerging trends and developments that promise to shape the trajectory of the industry in the years to come. From decentralized finance (DeFi) and non-fungible tokens (NFTs) to central bank digital currencies (CBDCs) and beyond, we paint a picture of a future where blockchain technology unlocks new possibilities and transforms the way we transact, invest, and interact with the world around us.

Whether you're a seasoned trader seeking to deepen your understanding of cryptocurrency or a curious newcomer eager to explore the possibilities of digital assets, "Cryptocurrency Unveiled" is your comprehensive guide to navigating the dynamic world of cryptocurrency with knowledge, confidence, and foresight. So, buckle up, dear reader, as we embark on an exhilarating journey through the world of cryptocurrency—one that promises to challenge your perceptions, expand your horizons, and unlock new opportunities on the horizon.

Chapter 1: What is Cryptocurrency?

Cryptocurrency represents a paradigm shift in the way we think about money and finance. In this chapter, we explore the fundamental concepts behind cryptocurrency, its origins, and its revolutionary potential to reshape the global financial landscape.

1. What is Cryptocurrency?: At its core, cryptocurrency is a digital or virtual form of currency that utilizes cryptography for secure and decentralized transactions. Unlike traditional fiat currencies issued and regulated by governments, cryptocurrency operates on decentralized networks, such as blockchain, which allows for peer-to-peer transactions without the need for intermediaries like banks or financial institutions.

2. Origins of Cryptocurrency: The concept of cryptocurrency traces back to the late 20th century, with early attempts to create digital currencies such as DigiCash and B-Money. However, it wasn't until the emergence of Bitcoin in 2009, with the publication of the Bitcoin whitepaper by the pseudonymous Satoshi Nakamoto, that cryptocurrency gained widespread attention and adoption. Bitcoin introduced the groundbreaking concept of a decentralized digital currency, based on a peer-to-peer network and cryptographic principles, laying the foundation for the entire cryptocurrency ecosystem.

3. How Cryptocurrency Works: Cryptocurrency transactions are recorded on a distributed ledger called a blockchain, which serves as a transparent and immutable record of all transactions. Each transaction is verified and added to the blockchain through a process called mining or validation, which relies on cryptographic algorithms and consensus mechanisms to ensure the integrity and security of the network. Participants in the network, known as miners or validators, use computational power to solve complex mathematical puzzles and validate transactions, in exchange for rewards in the form of newly minted cryptocurrency or transaction fees.

4. Key Features of Cryptocurrency: Cryptocurrency offers several key features that distinguish it from traditional forms of money:

Decentralization: Cryptocurrency operates on decentralized networks, meaning there is no central authority or governing body controlling the network. This decentralization ensures transparency, security, and censorship resistance, as no single entity has control over the network.

Security: Cryptocurrency transactions are secured through cryptographic techniques, making them resistant to fraud, counterfeiting, and tampering. Each transaction is cryptographically signed and recorded on the blockchain, providing a transparent and immutable record of ownership.

Anonymity and Privacy: While cryptocurrency transactions are pseudonymous, meaning they are not directly tied to real-world identities, they offer varying degrees of privacy and anonymity depending on the cryptocurrency and its underlying technology. Privacy-focused cryptocurrencies utilize advanced cryptographic techniques to enhance user privacy and confidentiality.

Borderless Transactions: Cryptocurrency transactions can be conducted across borders without the need for intermediaries, such as banks or financial institutions. This enables fast, cheap, and frictionless cross-border transactions, facilitating global trade and financial inclusion.

Chapter 2: Understanding Blockchain Technology

In this chapter, we dive deep into the revolutionary technology that underpins cryptocurrencies: blockchain. Understanding blockchain is essential as it forms the backbone of the entire cryptocurrency ecosystem, providing a decentralized and secure way to record transactions.

Blocks: At the core of blockchain technology are blocks. These blocks contain a bundle of transactions that are grouped together and verified by participants in the network. Each block is linked to the previous one through a cryptographic hash, forming an unbroken chain of blocks—hence the name "blockchain." This structure ensures the integrity and immutability of the transaction history, making it tamper-proof and resistant to manipulation.

Nodes: Blockchain networks consist of nodes, which are individual computers or devices connected to the network. These nodes play a crucial role in maintaining the integrity of the blockchain by validating and relaying transactions, as well as storing a copy of the entire blockchain ledger. The decentralized nature of blockchain means that no single entity controls the network, and transactions are verified by consensus among network participants.

Consensus Mechanisms: Consensus mechanisms are protocols that ensure all nodes in the network agree on the validity of transactions and the state of the blockchain. One of the most well-known consensus mechanisms is Proof of Work (PoW), used by Bitcoin and other cryptocurrencies, where miners compete to solve complex mathematical puzzles to validate transactions and create new blocks. Another common consensus mechanism is Proof of Stake (PoS), where validators are selected to create new blocks based on the amount of cryptocurrency they hold and are willing to "stake" as collateral.

Smart Contracts: Smart contracts are self-executing contracts with the terms of the agreement directly written into code. They automatically enforce the terms of the contract without the need for intermediaries, providing a trustless and transparent way to conduct transactions. Smart contracts run on blockchain platforms like Ethereum, enabling a wide range of decentralized applications (dApps) and programmable financial instruments.

Understanding these key components of blockchain technology is essential for grasping how cryptocurrencies operate and why they are considered secure and reliable forms of digital currency. Blockchain's decentralized and transparent nature not only revolutionizes finance but also has the potential to disrupt industries ranging from supply chain management to voting systems, unlocking new possibilities for efficiency, transparency, and trust in the digital age.

Chapter 3: Getting Started with Cryptocurrency

Getting started with cryptocurrency involves several crucial steps, and this chapter serves as your comprehensive guide to navigating the initial stages of your journey into the world of digital assets.

Choosing a Cryptocurrency Exchange: Cryptocurrency exchanges are online platforms where you can buy, sell, and trade digital assets. However, not all exchanges are created equal, and choosing the right one is paramount. Factors to consider include:

Security: Look for exchanges with robust security measures, such as encryption, two-factor authentication (2FA), and cold storage for funds.

Fees: Consider the fee structure of the exchange, including trading fees, deposit and withdrawal fees, and any other charges.

Supported Cryptocurrencies: Ensure that the exchange supports the cryptocurrencies you are interested in trading.

User Interface: Opt for exchanges with intuitive and user-friendly interfaces that make trading easy and accessible.

Setting Up a Wallet: A cryptocurrency wallet is a digital tool used to store, send, and receive cryptocurrencies securely. There are several types of wallets, each with its own advantages and security considerations:

Software Wallets: These are digital wallets that run on desktop, mobile, or web-based platforms. They are convenient but may be vulnerable to hacking if proper security measures are not taken.

Hardware Wallets: Hardware wallets are physical devices that store cryptocurrency keys offline, providing an extra layer of security against online threats. They are ideal for long-term storage of large amounts of cryptocurrency.

Paper Wallets: Paper wallets are physical documents that contain cryptocurrency keys printed or written on paper. They are considered one of the most secure forms of storage since they are not susceptible to online hacking.

When setting up a wallet, prioritize security by generating strong passwords, enabling 2FA, and keeping your private keys secure.

Securing Your Funds: Security is paramount in the world of cryptocurrency, where the irreversible nature of transactions makes safeguarding your funds essential. Implement security measures such as:

Enabling two-factor authentication (2FA) on all accounts associated with cryptocurrency trading.

Using strong, unique passwords and storing them securely using a password manager.

Keeping your private keys offline and securely backed up in multiple locations.

Being vigilant against phishing attacks and other forms of online fraud.

Chapter 4: Types of Cryptocurrencies

Cryptocurrency is a diverse and rapidly evolving ecosystem, with thousands of digital assets offering unique features, functionalities, and use cases. In this chapter, we explore the various types of cryptocurrencies beyond the pioneering Bitcoin, shedding light on the diverse array of digital assets that populate the cryptocurrency landscape.

1. Bitcoin (BTC): As the first and most well-known cryptocurrency, Bitcoin holds a special place in the cryptocurrency ecosystem. Introduced in 2009 by the pseudonymous Satoshi Nakamoto, Bitcoin was designed as a peer-to-peer electronic cash system, aiming to decentralize control over money and enable secure and transparent transactions. Bitcoin paved the way for the development of the entire cryptocurrency industry, inspiring the creation of thousands of alternative digital assets.

2. Altcoins: Altcoins, or alternative cryptocurrencies, encompass a wide range of digital assets that are alternatives to Bitcoin. These altcoins often offer improvements or variations on Bitcoin's technology, addressing limitations such as transaction speed, scalability, and privacy. Examples of popular altcoins include Ethereum (ETH), Litecoin (LTC), Ripple (XRP), and Bitcoin Cash (BCH). Altcoins may serve different purposes, such as providing a platform for decentralized applications (DApps), facilitating faster and cheaper transactions, or offering enhanced privacy features.

3. Tokens: Tokens are digital assets built on existing blockchain platforms, such as Ethereum or Binance Smart Chain. Unlike standalone cryptocurrencies like Bitcoin, tokens do not have their own blockchain but instead operate on existing blockchain networks as smart contracts. Tokens represent various assets, utilities, or rights and are often used in decentralized applications (DApps), initial coin offerings (ICOs), or tokenized assets such as real estate or digital collectibles. Examples of tokens include ERC-20 tokens on the Ethereum blockchain and BEP-20 tokens on the Binance Smart Chain.

4. Stablecoins: Stablecoins are a special category of cryptocurrencies that are designed to minimize price volatility by pegging their value to a stable asset, such as fiat currency (e.g., USD, EUR) or commodities (e.g., gold). Stablecoins provide a reliable medium of exchange and store of value in the volatile cryptocurrency market, offering stability and liquidity for traders and investors. Examples of stablecoins include Tether (USDT), USD Coin (USDC), and Dai (DAI).

5. Privacy Coins: Privacy coins are cryptocurrencies that prioritize user privacy and anonymity by implementing advanced cryptographic techniques to obfuscate transaction details and protect sensitive information. Privacy coins offer enhanced privacy features, such as ring signatures, stealth addresses, and zero-knowledge proofs, to ensure confidentiality and fungibility of transactions. Examples of privacy coins include Monero (XMR), Zcash (ZEC), and Dash (DASH).

Understanding the diverse landscape of cryptocurrencies allows investors and enthusiasts to explore different investment opportunities and participate in various blockchain ecosystems based on their interests and investment goals. Whether you're interested in the pioneering technology of Bitcoin, the programmable smart contracts of Ethereum, or the privacy-enhancing features of privacy coins, the world of cryptocurrency offers a wealth of opportunities for innovation, investment, and financial empowerment.

Chapter 5: How to Choose a Cryptocurrency Exchange

Choosing the right cryptocurrency exchange is essential for buying, selling, and trading digital assets securely and efficiently. This chapter provides guidance on evaluating exchanges based on the following factors:

Security Measures: Look for exchanges that prioritize security by implementing features such as two-factor authentication (2FA), cold storage of funds, and regular security audits. A reputable exchange should have a track record of safeguarding user funds and protecting against hacking incidents.

Fees and Commissions: Consider the trading fees, deposit and withdrawal fees, and any other charges associated with using the exchange. Compare fee structures across different exchanges to find a platform that offers competitive rates without sacrificing security or reliability.

Liquidity: Liquidity refers to the ease with which you can buy or sell assets on an exchange without affecting their price. Choose exchanges with high liquidity for popular trading pairs to ensure smooth execution of orders and minimal slippage.

Supported Cryptocurrencies: Check which cryptocurrencies are supported for trading on the exchange and ensure it offers the assets you're interested in buying or selling. Some exchanges may have a limited selection of cryptocurrencies, while others offer a wide range of options.

By considering these factors and conducting thorough research, readers can select a reputable cryptocurrency exchange that meets their trading needs and provides a secure and user-friendly trading experience.

Chapter 6: Setting Up Your Cryptocurrency Wallet

Cryptocurrency security is paramount in the digital landscape, where the decentralized and pseudonymous nature of transactions presents unique challenges and risks. In this chapter, we explore the fundamental principles of cryptocurrency security and risk management, equipping readers with the knowledge and tools to safeguard their digital assets effectively.

1. Secure Storage Solutions: Protecting cryptocurrency holdings begins with secure storage solutions. We delve into the various options available, including:

Hardware Wallets: Physical devices that store private keys offline, providing enhanced security against online threats such as hacking and malware.

Software Wallets: Digital wallets that run on desktop, mobile, or web-based platforms, offering convenience and accessibility but requiring robust security measures to protect against cyberattacks.

Paper Wallets: Physical documents containing cryptocurrency keys printed or written on paper, offering an offline storage solution that is immune to online hacking.

Understanding the strengths and limitations of each storage solution is essential for choosing the most appropriate option based on individual security preferences and risk tolerance.

2. Best Practices for Private Key Management: Private keys are the cryptographic keys that grant access to cryptocurrency holdings, and safeguarding them is critical for protecting digital assets. We explore best practices for private key management, including:

Generating Strong and Unique Keys: Using secure methods to generate strong and unique private keys that are resistant to brute-force attacks and hacking attempts.

Backup and Redundancy: Creating secure backups of private keys and storing them in multiple locations to prevent loss in the event of theft, damage, or hardware failure.

Cold Storage: Utilizing cold storage solutions, such as hardware wallets or paper wallets, to store private keys offline and minimize exposure to online threats.

By implementing robust private key management practices, individuals can mitigate the risk of unauthorized access and protect their cryptocurrency holdings from theft or loss.

3. Multi-Factor Authentication (MFA): Multi-factor authentication adds an extra layer of security to cryptocurrency accounts by requiring multiple forms of verification before granting access. We discuss the importance of enabling MFA on all accounts associated with cryptocurrency trading and investing and explore different authentication methods, such as SMS codes, authenticator apps, and hardware tokens.

4. Risk Management Strategies: Effective risk management is essential for navigating the volatile cryptocurrency market and minimizing potential losses. We examine risk management strategies such as:

Diversification: Spreading investments across multiple cryptocurrencies and asset classes to reduce exposure to any single risk factor or market volatility.

Position Sizing: Determining the appropriate allocation of funds to each investment based on risk tolerance and investment objectives.

Stop-Loss Orders: Using stop-loss orders to automatically sell cryptocurrency holdings if prices fall below predetermined levels, limiting potential losses and protecting investment capital.

By implementing these risk management strategies, traders and investors can mitigate downside risk and protect their portfolios from adverse market movements.

5. Staying Informed and Vigilant: Finally, we emphasize the importance of staying informed about the latest security threats and vulnerabilities in the cryptocurrency ecosystem and remaining vigilant against potential risks. This includes:

Monitoring Exchange Security: Keeping abreast of security measures implemented by cryptocurrency exchanges and choosing reputable platforms with robust security protocols.

Educating Yourself: Continuously educating oneself about cybersecurity best practices, emerging threats, and new developments in cryptocurrency security.

Exercising Caution: Exercising caution when interacting with unknown or suspicious entities, avoiding phishing scams, and practicing good cybersecurity hygiene to protect against social engineering attacks and online fraud.

Chapter 7: Buying and Selling Cryptocurrency

Buying and selling cryptocurrency is the primary activity in the cryptocurrency market, and understanding the nuances of this process is crucial for traders and investors. In this chapter, we explore the various aspects of buying and selling cryptocurrency, including different types of orders, market dynamics, and strategies for optimizing trading performance.

1. Market Orders: Market orders are the simplest type of order, executed at the current market price. When you place a market order, you are essentially instructing the exchange to buy or sell the specified cryptocurrency at the best available price. Market orders offer fast execution but may result in higher fees or price slippage, especially in volatile market conditions.

2. Limit Orders: Limit orders allow traders to set a specific price at which they are willing to buy or sell a cryptocurrency. Unlike market orders, limit orders are not executed immediately but are placed on the order book until the market price reaches the specified level. This gives traders more control over the execution price but may result in delayed order fulfillment if the market does not reach the desired price.

3. Stop-Loss Orders: Stop-loss orders are used to minimize losses by automatically selling a cryptocurrency if its price falls below a certain threshold. By setting a stop-loss order, traders can protect their investment from significant price declines and limit potential losses in volatile market conditions. Stop-loss orders are a crucial risk management tool for traders and investors, allowing them to mitigate downside risk while still participating in potential upside movements.

4. Take-Profit Orders: Take-profit orders are similar to stop-loss orders but are used to lock in profits when the price of a cryptocurrency reaches a certain level. By setting a take-profit order, traders can automatically sell their holdings at a predetermined price, ensuring that they capture gains from favorable price movements. Take-profit orders help traders capitalize on price fluctuations and maximize returns while minimizing emotional decision-making and timing errors.

5. Order Types: In addition to market and limit orders, cryptocurrency exchanges may offer advanced order types such as fill or kill (FOK), immediate or cancel (IOC), and trailing stop orders. These order types provide additional flexibility and customization options for traders, allowing them to fine-tune their trading strategies and optimize order execution in various market conditions.

Chapter 8: Security Measures for Cryptocurrency

Security is paramount in the world of cryptocurrency, where the irreversible nature of transactions and the prevalence of cyber threats pose significant risks to users' funds. This chapter provides essential security measures for protecting cryptocurrency holdings:

Secure Wallet Management: Use reputable cryptocurrency wallets with robust security features, such as encryption, multi-signature support, and hierarchical deterministic (HD) key generation. Choose wallets that allow users to control their private keys and avoid custodial services that hold users' funds on their behalf.

Two-Factor Authentication (2FA): Enable two-factor authentication (2FA) on all accounts associated with cryptocurrency trading and storage. 2FA adds an extra layer of security by requiring users to provide a second form of verification, such as a one-time password (OTP) generated by a mobile app or hardware token, in addition to their password.

Secure Password Management: Create strong, unique passwords for all cryptocurrency-related accounts and wallets and avoid using the same password across multiple platforms. Use a password manager to securely store and manage passwords and enable features like password autofill and password strength analysis to enhance security.

Phishing Awareness: Be vigilant against phishing attacks, where malicious actors attempt to trick users into disclosing sensitive information, such as login credentials or private keys, by impersonating legitimate websites or services. Verify the authenticity of websites and emails before providing any personal or financial information and use security features like browser extensions or email filters to detect and block phishing attempts.

Regular Software Updates: Keep cryptocurrency wallets, exchanges, and other software applications up to date with the latest security patches and updates to protect against known vulnerabilities and exploit attempts. Regularly review and audit security settings and configurations to ensure optimal protection against potential threats.

By implementing these security measures and staying informed about emerging threats and best practices, users can mitigate the risk of unauthorized access and safeguard their cryptocurrency holdings against theft, fraud, and other security breaches.

Chapter 9: Cryptocurrency Trading Strategies

Trading cryptocurrency requires a solid understanding of market dynamics and effective strategies to capitalize on price fluctuations and maximize profits. This chapter explores different trading approaches and techniques:

Long-Term Investing: Long-term investing involves buying and holding cryptocurrencies for an extended period, typically months or years, with the expectation that their value will increase over time. Long-term investors focus on fundamentals such as project team, technology, adoption, and market potential and are less concerned with short-term price fluctuations.

Short-Term Trading: Short-term trading involves buying and selling cryptocurrencies over shorter timeframes, such as days, hours, or even minutes, to capitalize on short-term price movements. Short-term traders rely on technical analysis, chart patterns, and market indicators to identify entry and exit points and make quick profits from price fluctuations.

Swing Trading: Swing trading combines elements of both long-term investing and short-term trading, aiming to capture gains from short to medium-term price swings within a broader trend. Swing traders use technical analysis to identify trading opportunities and employ risk management techniques such as stop-loss orders and position sizing to manage risk and maximize returns.

Day Trading: Day trading involves buying and selling cryptocurrencies within the same trading day, profiting from intraday price movements. Day traders rely on technical analysis, market news, and order flow analysis to identify short-term trading opportunities and execute quick trades to generate profits.

Arbitrage Trading: Arbitrage trading involves exploiting price differences between different cryptocurrency exchanges or trading pairs to generate profits with minimal risk. Arbitrage traders buy cryptocurrencies on one exchange where the price is lower and sell them on another exchange where the price is higher, profiting from the price discrepancy.

By understanding these trading strategies and techniques, traders can develop a personalized trading strategy that aligns with their investment goals, risk tolerance, and time horizon and improve their chances of success in the cryptocurrency market.

Chapter 10: Risks and Challenges in Cryptocurrency Trading

While cryptocurrency trading offers the potential for high returns, it also comes with inherent risks and challenges that traders must be aware of and manage effectively. This chapter examines various risks and challenges associated with cryptocurrency trading:

Market Volatility: Cryptocurrency markets are highly volatile, with prices subject to rapid and unpredictable fluctuations. Price volatility can lead to significant gains or losses in short periods, making it challenging to predict market movements accurately.

Regulatory Uncertainty: The regulatory landscape for cryptocurrency varies significantly from country to country and is subject to ongoing changes and updates. Regulatory uncertainty can impact market sentiment, liquidity, and trading volume and pose legal and compliance risks for traders and investors.

Exchange Hacks and Security Breaches: Cryptocurrency exchanges are prime targets for hacking attacks and security breaches, where hackers exploit vulnerabilities in exchange infrastructure to steal users' funds. Exchange hacks can result in significant financial losses and reputational damage and erode trust in the cryptocurrency ecosystem.

Liquidity Risks: Liquidity risk refers to the risk of not being able to buy or sell cryptocurrencies at desired prices due to insufficient trading volume or market depth. Illiquid markets can lead to price slippage, delayed order execution, and increased trading costs, particularly for large orders.

Technological Risks: Cryptocurrency transactions rely on complex technology infrastructure, including blockchain networks, wallets, and exchanges, which are susceptible to technical glitches, software bugs, and network congestion. Technological risks can disrupt trading activities, cause transaction delays, and result in financial losses for traders and investors.

By understanding these risks and challenges and implementing appropriate risk management strategies, such as diversification, position sizing, stop-loss orders, and portfolio rebalancing, traders can mitigate potential losses and navigate the cryptocurrency market more effectively.

Chapter 11: Regulatory Environment and Taxation

The regulatory landscape and taxation surrounding cryptocurrency are crucial aspects that traders and investors must navigate. In this chapter, we explore the evolving regulatory environment for cryptocurrency and its implications for market participants.

1. Regulatory Frameworks: The regulatory landscape for cryptocurrency varies significantly from country to country and is subject to ongoing changes and updates. Some jurisdictions have embraced cryptocurrency and blockchain technology, implementing clear regulatory guidelines and frameworks to promote innovation and protect investors. Others have adopted a more cautious approach, imposing restrictions or outright bans on cryptocurrency trading and usage. Understanding the regulatory framework in your jurisdiction is essential for ensuring compliance and mitigating legal and compliance risks.

2. Compliance Requirements: Traders and investors must be aware of and comply with relevant regulatory requirements and obligations, such as registration, licensing, reporting, and taxation. Failure to comply with regulatory requirements can result in legal and financial consequences, including fines, penalties, and even criminal prosecution. It's essential to stay informed about regulatory developments and seek legal advice when necessary to ensure compliance with applicable laws and regulations.

3. Taxation: Cryptocurrency taxation is a complex and evolving area that varies depending on factors such as jurisdiction, asset type, and transaction type. Tax authorities in many countries consider cryptocurrency to be a taxable asset subject to capital gains tax, income tax, or other forms of taxation. Traders and investors are responsible for accurately reporting their cryptocurrency transactions and paying applicable taxes to avoid penalties and legal consequences. It's essential to keep detailed records of cryptocurrency transactions, including dates, amounts, and transaction details, to facilitate accurate tax reporting and compliance.

4. Regulatory Evolution: As cryptocurrency adoption continues to grow, regulatory authorities and policymakers are grappling with how to balance innovation and consumer protection and mitigate risks associated with cryptocurrency trading and usage. Regulatory evolution is expected to continue as governments and regulatory bodies adapt to the evolving cryptocurrency landscape and develop clear and comprehensive regulatory frameworks to promote innovation, protect investors, and ensure financial

stability. Traders and investors must stay informed about regulatory developments and engage with policymakers and industry stakeholders to advocate for sensible and effective regulation that fosters innovation while safeguarding investor interests.

Chapter 12: The Future of Cryptocurrency

The future of cryptocurrency is full of promise and potential, with continued innovation and adoption driving growth and transformation across various industries. This chapter explores emerging trends and developments in the cryptocurrency space and their implications for the future:

Decentralized Finance (DeFi): Decentralized finance (DeFi) is a rapidly growing sector within the cryptocurrency ecosystem that aims to decentralize traditional financial services such as lending, borrowing, trading, and asset management. DeFi platforms leverage blockchain technology to create open and permissionless financial infrastructure, enabling users to access financial services without intermediaries.

Non-Fungible Tokens (NFTs): Non-fungible tokens (NFTs) are unique digital assets that represent ownership or proof of authenticity of digital or physical items such as artwork, collectibles, and virtual real estate. NFTs have gained popularity as a means of tokenizing and trading digital assets, enabling creators and collectors to monetize and exchange digital content in new and innovative ways.

Central Bank Digital Currencies (CBDCs): Central bank digital currencies (CBDCs) are digital versions of fiat currencies issued and regulated by central banks. CBDCs aim to modernize and streamline the existing monetary system, providing faster, cheaper, and more inclusive payment solutions while maintaining central bank control over monetary policy and financial stability.

Scalability and Interoperability: Scalability and interoperability are critical challenges facing the cryptocurrency ecosystem as it seeks to achieve mainstream adoption and scale to accommodate growing demand. Solutions such as layer 2 scaling solutions, cross-chain interoperability protocols, and blockchain interoperability frameworks are being developed to address these challenges and enhance the scalability, efficiency, and usability of cryptocurrency networks.

Regulatory Evolution: As cryptocurrency adoption continues to grow, regulatory authorities and policymakers are grappling with how to balance innovation and consumer protection and mitigate risks associated with cryptocurrency trading and usage. Regulatory evolution is expected to continue as governments and regulatory bodies adapt to the evolving cryptocurrency landscape and develop clear and comprehensive regulatory frameworks to promote innovation, protect investors, and ensure financial stability.

Conclusion

In conclusion, "Cryptocurrency Unveiled: An Introductory Guide to Understanding and Trading Digital Assets" has provided readers with a comprehensive overview of the world of cryptocurrency. Throughout the book, we have explored the fundamentals of cryptocurrency, delved into the intricacies of blockchain technology, and provided practical guidance for getting started with cryptocurrency trading.

We began by defining cryptocurrency and discussing its decentralized nature, cryptographic security, and revolutionary potential. We then explored blockchain technology, the underlying technology that powers cryptocurrencies, and its key components such as blocks, nodes, and consensus mechanisms. Armed with this foundational knowledge, readers gained a deeper understanding of how cryptocurrencies operate and why they are considered secure and reliable forms of digital currency.

Moving forward, we guided readers through the process of getting started with cryptocurrency, from choosing a reputable exchange to setting up a secure wallet. We explored the different types of cryptocurrencies available, including Bitcoin, altcoins, and tokens, and provided guidance on selecting the right exchange and wallet to meet their trading needs.

We then delved into the intricacies of cryptocurrency trading, discussing different trading strategies and techniques, such as long-term investing, swing trading, and day trading. We also examined the risks and challenges associated with cryptocurrency trading, including market volatility, regulatory uncertainty, and security threats, and provided strategies for mitigating these risks and maximizing returns.

Throughout the book, we emphasized the importance of security and compliance in the world of cryptocurrency, providing essential security measures for protecting cryptocurrency holdings and discussing regulatory frameworks and taxation requirements. We also explored emerging trends and developments in the cryptocurrency space, such as decentralized finance (DeFi), non-fungible tokens (NFTs), and central bank digital currencies (CBDCs), and their implications for the future of finance and technology.

As readers conclude their journey through the world of cryptocurrency, we encourage them to continue exploring and learning about this exciting and rapidly evolving industry. Whether you're a seasoned trader or someone entirely new to cryptocurrency, there's always something new to discover and opportunities to seize in this dynamic and transformative space.

Remember, the key to success in cryptocurrency trading lies in knowledge, diligence, and perseverance. Stay informed, stay curious, and embrace the opportunities that await in the world of cryptocurrency. Happy trading!

Glossary

1. Cryptocurrency: A digital or virtual form of currency that utilizes cryptographic techniques for secure and decentralized transactions. Cryptocurrencies operate on distributed ledger technology, such as blockchain, and are not controlled by any central authority.

2. Blockchain: A decentralized and distributed ledger technology that records transactions across multiple computers in a tamper-resistant and transparent manner. Each transaction is verified and added to a block, which is then linked to the previous block, forming an unbroken chain of blocks.

3. Bitcoin: The first and most well-known cryptocurrency, created by the pseudonymous Satoshi Nakamoto in 2009. Bitcoin operates on a decentralized peer-to-peer network and is used for secure and transparent transactions without the need for intermediaries.

4. Altcoin: Any cryptocurrency other than Bitcoin. Altcoins may offer variations or improvements on Bitcoin's technology and include cryptocurrencies such as Ethereum, Ripple, Litecoin, and Bitcoin Cash.

5. Token: A digital asset issued on an existing blockchain platform, such as Ethereum. Tokens represent various assets, utilities, or rights and are often

used in decentralized applications (DApps), initial coin offerings (ICOs), or tokenized assets such as real estate or digital collectibles.

6. Wallet: A digital tool used to store, send, and receive cryptocurrencies securely. Wallets come in various forms, including hardware wallets, software wallets, and paper wallets, each offering different levels of security and convenience.

7. Mining: The process of validating and adding transactions to a blockchain by solving complex mathematical puzzles. Miners compete to find the solution to a cryptographic puzzle and are rewarded with newly minted cryptocurrency or transaction fees for their efforts.

8. Consensus Mechanism: A protocol used to achieve agreement among participants in a blockchain network on the validity of transactions and the state of the blockchain. Common consensus mechanisms include Proof of Work (PoW), Proof of Stake (PoS), and Delegated Proof of Stake (DPoS).

9. Smart Contract: Self-executing contracts with the terms of the agreement directly written into code. Smart contracts automatically enforce the terms of the contract without the need for intermediaries, providing a trustless and transparent way to conduct transactions.

10. Decentralized Finance (DeFi): A movement that aims to recreate traditional financial systems using blockchain technology to enable decentralized and permissionless financial services, such as lending, borrowing, and trading, without the need for intermediaries.

11. Non-Fungible Token (NFT): A unique digital asset that represents ownership of a specific item or piece of content, such as digital art, collectibles, or virtual real estate. NFTs are indivisible and cannot be

exchanged on a like-for-like basis, unlike fungible cryptocurrencies such as Bitcoin or Ethereum.

12. Stablecoin: A type of cryptocurrency designed to minimize price volatility by pegging its value to a stable asset, such as fiat currency (e.g., USD, EUR) or commodities (e.g., gold). Stablecoins provide stability and liquidity in the cryptocurrency market, facilitating transactions and serving as a reliable store of value.

13. Cold Storage: A method of storing cryptocurrency offline, typically on hardware wallets or paper wallets, to minimize exposure to online threats such as hacking and malware. Cold storage provides enhanced security for long-term storage of cryptocurrency holdings.

14. Multi-factor Authentication (MFA): A security mechanism that requires users to provide multiple forms of verification before granting access to an account or platform. MFA enhances security by adding an extra layer of protection against unauthorized access and cyberattacks.

15. Private Key: A cryptographic key that grants access to cryptocurrency holdings and enables transactions on a blockchain network. Private keys must be kept secure and confidential to prevent unauthorized access to digital assets.

Resources

1. Books:

"Mastering Bitcoin" by Andreas M. Antonopoulos: A comprehensive guide to Bitcoin and blockchain technology, covering technical concepts, decentralized networks, and cryptocurrency fundamentals.

"The Internet of Money" series by Andreas M. Antonopoulos: A collection of books that explore the social, economic, and philosophical implications of cryptocurrency and blockchain technology.

"Blockchain Basics: A Non-Technical Introduction in 25 Steps" by Daniel Drescher: An accessible introduction to blockchain technology, covering its history, applications, and potential impact on various industries.

2. Online Courses:

Coursera: Offers a range of courses on cryptocurrency, blockchain technology, and related topics, including "Bitcoin and Cryptocurrency Technologies" and "Blockchain Basics."

Udemy: Provides numerous courses on cryptocurrency trading, investing, and technical analysis, as well as blockchain development and smart contract programming.

Khan Academy: Offers educational resources on cryptocurrency and blockchain technology, covering topics such as cryptography, mining, and decentralized networks.

3. Websites and Blogs:

CoinDesk: A leading source of news, analysis, and information on cryptocurrency and blockchain technology, featuring articles, research reports, and market data.

CoinTelegraph: Another popular cryptocurrency news website, offering a wide range of articles, opinion pieces, and analysis on the latest trends and developments in the crypto space.

Ethereum Blog: The official blog of the Ethereum project, providing updates, announcements, and insights into the world's leading smart contract platform.

4. Forums and Communities:

Reddit: Subreddits such as r/CryptoCurrency, r/Bitcoin, and r/Ethereum serve as hubs for discussion, news, and information sharing among cryptocurrency enthusiasts and investors.

Bitcointalk: A popular cryptocurrency forum featuring discussions on Bitcoin, altcoins, mining, trading, and technical development.

Discord and Telegram: Many cryptocurrency projects and communities have active Discord servers and Telegram groups where members can interact, ask questions, and share insights in real-time.

5. Podcasts:

"Unchained" by Laura Shin: A leading podcast covering cryptocurrency, blockchain technology, and decentralized finance, featuring interviews with industry experts and thought leaders.

"The Pomp Podcast" by Anthony Pompliano: A podcast exploring the intersection of finance, technology, and cryptocurrency, featuring discussions on investing, entrepreneurship, and macroeconomic trends.

"Epicenter" by Brian Fabian Crain and Sebastien Couture: A podcast featuring in-depth interviews and discussions with leading figures in the cryptocurrency and blockchain space.

These resources provide a wealth of information and insights for individuals interested in learning more about cryptocurrency, blockchain technology, and related topics. Whether you're a beginner looking to understand the basics or an experienced enthusiast seeking advanced knowledge, these resources offer valuable opportunities for education and exploration in the dynamic world of digital assets.

www.ingramcontent.com/pod-product-compliance
Lightning Source LLC
Chambersburg PA
CBHW050035230526
45470CB00003B/1288